CREATIVE ENERGY

CREATIVE ENERGY

BEARING WITNESS

FOR THE EARTH

Thomas Berry

SIERRA CLUB BOOKS · SAN FRANCISCO

A Sierra Club Pathstone Edition™

The Sierra Club, founded in 1892 by John Muir, has devoted itself to the study and protection of the earth's scenic and ecological resources—mountains, wetlands, woodlands, wild shores and rivers, deserts and plains. The publishing program of the Sierra Club offers books to the public as a non-profit educational service in the hope that they may enlarge the public's understanding of the Club's basic concerns. The point of view expressed in each book, however, does not necessarily represent that of the Club. The Sierra Club has some sixty chapters coast to coast, in Canada, Hawaii, and Alaska. For information about how you may participate in its programs to preserve wilderness and the quality of life, please address inquiries to Sierra Club, 730 Polk Street, San Francisco, CA 94109.

This volume in the Sierra Club Pathstone series comprises chapters 4, 10, 15, and 16 of *The Dream of the Earth.*

Library of Congress Cataloging-in-Publication Data

Berry, Thomas Mary, 1914–
[Dream of the earth. Selections]
Creative energy / Thomas Berry.
p.   cm.
" . . . comprises chapters 4, 10, 15, and 16 of
The dream of the earth"—T.p. verso.
ISBN 0-87156-854-3 (paper : alk. paper)
1. Human ecology—Religious aspects.   2. Nature—Religious aspects.
3. Human ecology—Philosophy.   I. Title.
GF80.B4725   1996
304.2—dc20   95-44234

Production by Susan Ristow · Cover and book design by Amy Evans
Composition by Wilsted & Taylor

Printed in the United States of America on acid-free paper containing a minimum of 50% recovered waste paper, of which at least 10% of the fiber content is post-consumer waste

10   9   8   7   6   5   4   3   2   1

CONTENTS

CREATIVE
ENERGY

·⚜·

A WARENESS OF AN all-pervading mysterious energy articulated in the infinite variety of natural phenomena seems to be the primordial experience of human consciousness, awakening to an awesome universe filled with mysterious power. Not only is energy our primary experience; energy, and its multiple modes of expression, is also the primary concern of modern physics, its ultimate term of reference in describing the most fundamental reality of the universe. Physics is establishing contact with energy events rather than with substances of atomic or subatomic dimensions. These energy events extend in size all the way from subatomic particles to galactic systems. The universe can be seen as a single, if multiform, energy event, just as a particle such as the photon is itself perceived in its historical reality as an energy event.

Belief in a personal creative energy principle is the primary basis of Western spiritual tradition. Thus the creed opens with a reference to power as the distinguishing attribute of the creative principle of heaven and earth and all things. Unfortunately Western religious traditions have been so occupied with redemptive healing of a flawed world that they tend to ignore creation as it is experienced in our times. Consequently one of the basic difficulties of the modern West is its division into a secular scientific community, which is concerned with creative energies, and a religious community, which is concerned with redemptive energies. So concerned are we with redemptive healing that once healed, we look only to be more healed. We seldom get to our functional role within the creative intentions of the universe.

In an earlier phase of human development, creation mythologies provided the basic context for personal and social existence. In accord with these great mythic statements, the various cultural forms were established. These cultural forms themselves were energy expressions recognized primarily as subjective and psychic rather than physical in nature. The truly great society was the society of the divine, the natural, and the human. Each of these communicated energy to and evoked energy from the others. The Great Wheel turned, the Great Cosmic Wheel of the universe.

Within this context the human community was energized by the cosmic rituals wherein ultimate meaning was attained, absolute mysteries were enacted, human needs were fulfilled. An abundance of energy flowed into the human when these monumental celebrations took place; human psychic transformation found its proper instrument and expression. The variety of human societies was formed.

This was the archetypal period of history, the divine age of Vico, the period when the great goddesses and gods emerged in human consciousness; the imaginative powers attained heights never again to be rivaled. The pyramids were built. The Ming T'ang palace of the Chinese took shape. The Parthenon gave expression to the serene depths of the Greek mind. The Mayan and Aztec altars were raised. Borobodur rose majestically into the Indonesian sky.

Here was energy on a vast scale. We hardly know whether to refer to it as divine or cosmic or human energy. It was in reality one energy shared by all three in terms of subjective attribution. Primarily a numinous psychic energy, it found expression not only in monumental architecture, but also in the hierarchical structure of the great societies. Ritual codes were established on a firm basis. The human venture moved into the larger phase of its own structuring. *The Book of Ritual* of the Chinese was composed, and the *Code of Manu* in India. These ritual codes were the main instruments for sustaining and channeling the energies needed by the community.

In all of these societies spiritual movements took place, indicating that the ritual celebrations and the codes of conduct needed to be supplemented by an interior intensity equal to the elaborate exterior enactments. At the center and along the margins of these classical ritual civilizations, spiritual movements appeared in order to intensify the energy resources of both the individual and the society and to enable them to function in a properly human mode. To maintain these spiritual movements required a personal presence that only the most disciplined personalities with almost unlimited interior power could fulfill. Thus the sages, rishis, yogis, gurus, priests, philosophers, prophets, heroes, and divine kings of antiquity: Confucius, Buddha, Ignathon, Moses, Isaiah, Darius, Ch'in Shih Huang Ti, Asoka, Plato, Christ, and, later, Mohammed. These archetypal personalities have been followed by an unending sequence of others who have been instrumental in keeping the energy level of the various civilizations sufficient to carry on the basic functions required for their continuance.

These ancient ritual patterns and the personal spiritual disciplines were sufficient to keep the great societies within their proper energy cycles. Because entropy made itself felt and a running down of the system was experienced, a new world age was periodically inaugurated. All that was diminished was made new and full and vigorous at the annual new year or springtime festivals.

During the period of classical cultures, this basic energy structure continued. Classical culture itself was a kind of energy pulsating in and through sacred liturgies carried out in seasonal life periods, as well as in the personal life cycle from birth to maturity to death. There was no functional awareness of an irreversibly unfolding universe within developmental historical time. The basic pattern of existence was experienced as movement and change within a contained and seasonally renewed world. Things might pass through multiple forms, but those forms of the real were themselves fixed in their structure.

There was a basic consistency in all of this that was not radically disrupted until the modern period when the entire order of things was shaken by the new historical mode of thinking the world. The true reality of things, and even the universal and liberating goal of human striving, came to be seen as a development within the historical process. This process was seen not as the set alteration of the seasons or as adjustment to any established structure of the natural or the social order. The world was a one-time emerging world. There was no established cosmos, no abiding society, only a cosmogenesis and a sociogenesis. The evocation of energies continued within the ancient patterns, but these patterns themselves came to be interpreted within a new historical context.

A new axis for the expression of energy was created. The emphasis shifted from the seasonal rhythms of the universe and from the transcendent liberation experiences to a shaping of the time process toward some ultimate fulfillment within the historical order. This new sense of a shape and destiny to be progressively realized within the historical order would ultimately bring about the most significant energy revolution that has taken place in the human process from its earliest phases. The story of how this has taken place is the story of Western civilization, even the story of the human community.

The destinies not only of the human, but also of

the earth itself, were to be determined by this shift in the energy system of the human enterprise. The very purpose of this new energy was not to maintain the existing system nor to spiritually transcend the natural systems, but to change the system itself in its deepest meaning and the entire modality of its functioning. While significant changes had already taken place in the rise of the various civilizational developments, none of these was capable of affecting the structure and functioning of the earth in such a decisive manner.

Although this new vision was first set forth in the prophetic writings and in the apocalyptic visions of Daniel, it found its most effective presentation in the Revelation of John the Divine, especially in his reference to the "millennium," the thousand years at the end of the historical process when the great dragon would be chained up, when peace and justice would appear, and when the human condition would be decisively surmounted. This millennial vision is the source of what may be the most powerful psychic energies ever released on the earth, psychic energies that have eventually taken extensive control over the physical functioning of the planet and are now entering into control of its biological systems.

This vision at first concerned only the spiritual development of the human community. The natural world remained an unchanging world. Then, with the development of the empirical sciences, a new sense of historical process emerged. First the human mind was experienced as being perfected over the centuries. Then the earth itself was perceived as the product of an evolutionary sequence of changes. In the nineteenth century, through Lamarck, Darwin, and Wallace, the biosystems of the earth were seen as evolutionary processes. Finally, in the twentieth century, the universe revealed itself as an emergent evolutionary process, not as cosmos, but as cosmogenesis.

This in itself might not have been so revolutionary in its consequences were it not for the entrancing vision of a future millennial fulfillment beyond the human condition. When this vision of the future was joined with a feeling of the surging energies of the galactic systems, with the earth-shaping powers, and with the irrepressible fecundity of life in all its forms, then we were simultaneously propelled by the past and drawn by the future in such absolute fashion that resistance would have been the last absurdity.

There is a difference, however, between this impetus from the past and the attraction of the future. The movement of the universe from its first fiery stages, through its various transformations, on to the earth, life, and to our human mode of being, is beyond our control. Even in our earlier civilizational phases we were following a somewhat instinctive process of our development. We had minimal control over the natural world or over our own lives. But now this has changed.

With our new knowledge we can participate more fully in the emergent processes of the present and the shaping of the future. Yet the primary determinant in our activities is our sense of millennial fulfillment in whatever form it presents itself. In the last few centuries the millennium has appeared as the Enlightenment, the democratic age, the nation-state, the classless society, the capitalist age of peace and plenty, and the industrial wonderworld.

It is a supreme irony of history that the consequences of these millennial expectations have been the devastation of the planet—wasteworld rather than wonderworld. Of special significance is the fact that these entrancements and the consequent devastation exist on a worldwide scale. The earth entire and the human community are bound in a single destiny, and that destiny just now has a disintegrating aspect. The disintegration is so threatening because both the psychic and the physical energy levels were so high, the consequences generally irreversible. The modern question has always been the control of energy that exists on an order of magnitude many times greater than what was available in prior periods of history. Whatever the direction taken by the human community in modern times, its consequences will be vast beyond the imagining of any former generations. That we ourselves see only the immediate microphase consequences of our energy systems and almost completely miss the larger, macrophase, consequences of these systems is an indication of our need to be extremely cautious in any use of the energies available to us.

The industrial context in which we presently function cannot be changed significantly in the immediate future. Our immediate survival is bound up in this context, with all its beneficial as well as its destructive aspects. What is needed, however, is a comprehensive change in the control and direction of the energies available to us. Most of all we need to alter our commitment from an industrial wonderworld achieved by plundering processes to an integral earth community based on a mutually enhancing human-earth relationship. This move from an anthropocentric sense of reality and value to a biocentric norm is essential.

The ideal of a human habitat within a natural setting of trees and fields and flowering plants, of flowing streams and seacoasts and those living forms that swim through the waters and move over the land and fly through the air—a world of nontoxic rain and noncontaminated wells, of unpolluted seacoasts with their fertile wetlands—the ideal of a human community integral with such a setting, if properly understood with all the severity of its demands on its human occupants, would seem to be our only effective way into a sustainable and humanly satisfying future.

This is, of course, a mythic vision, highly romanticized if it is taken too literally. Yet it is considerably less idealized than the wonderworld vision that supports our present industrial system. In both cases we recognize that the mythic vision is what evokes the energies needed to sustain the human effort involved. The important thing is that the mythic vision lead to a sustainable context for the survival and continued evolution of the earth and its living forms. The ecological vision that we are proposing is the only context that is consistent with the evolutionary processes that brought the earth and all its living beings into that state of florescence that existed prior to the industrial age. Because this earlier situation made serious demands upon the human in return for the benefits given, the industrial age was invented to avoid the return due for the benefits received. The burdens imposed upon the human in its natural setting, generally referred to as the human condition, established a situation unacceptable to an anthropocentric community with its deep psychic resentment against any such demands imposed upon it, hence the entire effort of the industrial society to transform the natural world into total subservience.

So effective has this been that only fragments of this earlier natural world survive, and those are being extinguished at an astonishing rate each day, even though the industrial world itself cannot sustain itself apart from the resources taken from the very same natural world. Even so, a deep psychic fixation exists that inhibits any effort at mitigating this destructive process. So far, the energy evoked by the ecological vision has not been sufficient to offset the energies evoked by the industrial vision—even when its desolation becomes so obvious as it is at the present time. The various peoples of the earth find themselves caught between a dissolving industrial economy and a ruined natural environment. Immediate survival seems to be with the pervasive industrial processes.

Millennial expectations are reduced to endurance in a desolated natural world.

Yet the psychic energies sustaining the industrial illusion are now dissolving in confrontation with the problems of water for drinking, air for breathing, nontoxic soil for food production. A new energy is beginning to appear. Already a pervasive influence throughout the North American continent, this energy is finding expression in more than ten thousand ecologically oriented action groups on this continent; it is distributed through all the professions and through all the various forms of economic, political, educational, religious, literary, and media enterprise.

If this movement has not yet achieved its full efficacy in confrontation with the industrial vision, it is not primarily because of the economic or political realities of the situation, but because of the mythic power of the industrial vision. Even when its consequences in a desolate planet are totally clear, the industrial order keeps its control over human activities because of the energy generated by the mythic quality of its vision. We could describe our industrial society as counterproductive, addictive, paralyzing, manifestation of a deep cultural pathology. Mythic addictions function something like alcohol and drug addictions. Even when they are obviously destroying the addicted person, the psychic fixation does not permit any change, in the hope that continued addiction will at least permit momentary survival. Any effective cure requires passing through the agonies of withdrawal. If such withdrawal is an exceptional achievement in individual lives, we can only guess at the difficulty on the civilizational or even the global scale.

Advances in ecological activities can be observed throughout every continent at the present time. The World Charter for Nature was approved by the United Nations Assembly in 1982. The World Strategy for Conservation and Development was drawn up and approved in 1980 by more than seven hundred scientists from more than one hundred different nations. A variety of projects are being initiated in Europe, Asia, Africa, and South America, as well as in North America. The way is now clear. In North America the directions have been established in all the basic professions and activities. In economics, energy, food production, law, medicine, education, religion, ethics—in every aspect of life—the ecological pattern of functioning is now established. What is needed presently is more-adequate elaboration of the mythic phase of the ecological process.

As has been mentioned, the main difficulty in re-placing the industrial order is not the physical nature of the situation, but its psychic entrancement. This mythic commitment preceded the actuality of the in-dustrial achievement. It was, rather, a condition for, not the consequence of, the industrial achievement. So, too, with the ecological pattern: the myth is pri-mary, although its early realization must be achieved and valid indications established of its possibilities for the future. A taste for existence within the function-ing of the natural world is urgent. Without a fasci-nation with the grandeur of the North American continent, the energy needed for its preservation will never be developed. Something more than the utili-tarian aspect of fresh water must be evoked if we are ever to have water with the purity required for our survival. There must be a mystique of the rain if we are ever to restore the purity of the rainfall.

This evocation of mystique is the role that is ful-filled by the poets and natural history essayists. In a country such as the Philippines, which is being devas-tated, where the rain forests are being eliminated, the soil eroded, the mangrove swamps destroyed, the coral reefs blasted, the streams polluted, there is a primary need to strengthen the mystique of the land. If a mystique of the land existed in some instinctive manner in the past, it is no longer sufficient. Beyond the country's political and economic needs, and possibly a prior condition for any sustainable political structure or functional economy, is the need for a mystique of the land such as is supplied by the nature poets, essayists, and artists; for educators and religious teachers with a sense of the islands as revelation of the divine; for lawyers with a sense of the inherent rights of natural beings. The mythic dimension, the sacred aspect of the Philippines, is needed if anything significant is to be done to remedy the devastation already present and to activate a program of renewal. Only in a viable natural world can there be a viable human world.

In every country, then, a mystique of the land is needed to counter the industrial mystique. This mystique must be associated with the three basic commitments of our times: commitment to the earth as irreversible process, to the ecological age as the only viable form of the millennial ideal, and to a sense of progress that includes the natural as well as the human world. Only by fulfilling these conditions can we evoke the energies that are needed for future survival in a setting of mutually enhancing human-earth relationships.

The mythic dimension of the ecological age is neither a romanticism nor an idealism. It is rather a deep insight into the structure and functioning of the entire earth process. This includes its seasonal rhythms as well as its historical transformations, its global coherence as well as its bioregional diversity, its revelatory communication as well as its pragmatic functioning. The revelatory aspect of the ecological age finds expression in the ecological archetype which finds its most effective expression in the great story of the universe.

This story presents the organic unity and creative power of the planet Earth as they are expressed in the symbol of the Great Mother; the evolutionary process through which every living form achieves its identity and its proper role in the universal drama as it is expressed in the symbol of the Great Journey; the relatedness of things in an omnicentered universe as expressed by the mandala; the sequence of moments whereby each reality fulfills its role of sacrificial disintegration in order that new and more highly differentiated forms might appear as expressed by the transformational symbols; and, finally, the symbols of a complex organism with roots, trunk, branches, and leaves, which indicate the coherence and functional efficacy of the entire organism, as expressed by the Cosmic Tree and the Tree of Life.

These archetypal symbols are the main instruments for the evocation of the energies needed for our future renewal of the earth. They provide not only the understanding and the sense of direction that we need, they also evoke the energy needed to create this new situation. This energy must be of a unique order of magnitude, since never before has the planet or the human community been confronted with questions of ultimacy supported by such a powerful mythology and combined with such capacity for exploiting the natural world. It needs to be repeated continually that we are not now dealing with another historical change or cultural modification such as those that have been experienced in the past. The changes we are dealing with are changes on a geological and biological order of magnitude. The four great components of the earth—the landsphere, the watersphere, the airsphere, and the lifesphere—are being decisively and permanently altered in their composition and their functioning by the more recent sphere, the mindsphere, altered, that is, in a deleterious, irreversible manner.

Here we need to realize that the ultimate custody

of the earth belongs to the earth. The issues we are considering are fundamentally earth issues that need to be dealt with in some direct manner by the earth itself. As humans we need to recognize the limitations in our capacity to deal with these comprehensive issues of the earth's functioning. So long as we are under the illusion that we know best what is good for the earth and for ourselves, then we will continue our present course, with its devastating consequences on the entire earth community.

Our best procedure might be to consider that we need not a human answer to an earth problem, but an earth answer to an earth problem. The earth will solve its problems, and possibly our own, if we will let the earth function in its own ways. We need only listen to what the earth is telling us.

THE NEW STORY

·～❧～·

I T'S ALL A QUESTION of story. We are in trouble
just now because we do not have a good story. We
are in between stories. The old story, the account of
how the world came to be and how we fit into it, is no
longer effective. Yet we have not learned the new
story. Our traditional story of the universe sustained
us for a long period of time. It shaped our emotional
attitudes, provided us with life purposes, and energized action. It consecrated suffering and integrated
knowledge. We awoke in the morning and knew
where we were. We could answer the questions of
our children. We could identify crime, punish trans-
gressors. Everything was taken care of because the
story was there. It did not necessarily make people
good, nor did it take away the pains and stupidities of
life or make for unfailing warmth in human associa-

tion. It did provide a context in which life could function in a meaningful manner.

Presently this traditional story is dysfunctional in its larger social dimensions, even though some believe it firmly and act according to its guidance. Aware of the dysfunctional aspects of the traditional program, some persons have moved on into different, often new-age, orientations, which have consistently proved ineffective in dealing with our present life situation. Even with advanced science and technology, with superb techniques in manufacturing and commerce, in communications and computation, our secular society remains without satisfactory meaning or the social discipline needed for a life leading to emotional, aesthetic, and spiritual fulfillment. Because of this lack of satisfaction many persons are returning to a religious fundamentalism. But that, too, can be seen as inadequate to supply the values for sustaining our needed social discipline.

A radical reassessment of the human situation is needed, especially concerning those basic values that give to life some satisfactory meaning. We need something that will supply in our times what was supplied formerly by our traditional religious story. If we are to achieve this purpose, we must begin where everything begins in human affairs—with the basic story, our narrative of how things came to be, how they came to be as they are, and how the future can be given some satisfying direction. We need a story that will educate us, a story that will heal, guide, and discipline us.

Western society did have, in its traditional story of the universe, an agreed-upon functioning story up until somewhere around the fourteenth century. This religion-based story originated in a revelatory experience some three thousand years ago. According to this story, the original harmony of the universe was broken by a primordial human fault, and that necessitated formation of a believing redemptive community that would take shape through the course of time. Human history was moving infallibly toward its fulfillment in the peace of a reconstituted paradise.

This religious story was integrated with the Ptolemaic account of the universe and how it functioned, an abiding universe that endlessly renewed itself and its living forms through the seasonal sequence of time. The introduction of irreversible historical time onto this abiding cosmological scene is precisely the contribution of the Western religious tradition. However severe the turbulent moments of history through the late classical and early medieval periods, these at least took place within a secure natural world and within a fixed context of interpretation. Whatever the problems were, they were not problems concerning the basic human or spiritual values that were at stake. Those were clear.

The confusion and insecurity that we presently experience originated, to a large extent, in the fourteenth century when Europe experienced the plague known as the Black Death. Without making this event a simplistic explanation of all later history, we can say that it was a transition period. Even more, it was a central traumatic moment in Western history. It is estimated that this plague, which reached Europe in 1347, had by 1349 killed off perhaps one-third of the population. Almost half of the people of Florence died within a three-month period. Throughout the later fourteenth century there was a population decline in the whole of Europe. In London the last of the great plagues was in 1665.

In response to the plague and to other social disturbances of the fourteenth and fifteenth centuries, two directions of development can be identified— one toward a religious redemption out of the tragic world, the other toward greater control of the physical world to escape its pain and to increase its utility to human society. From these two tendencies the two dominant cultural communities of recent centuries were formed: the believing religious community and the secular community with its new scientific knowledge and its industrial powers of exploiting the natural world.

Since the people of these centuries had no knowledge of germs and thus no explanation of the plague, other than divine judgment on a wicked world, the answers most generally sought were in the moral and spiritual order, frequently outside the orthodox teachings of the church. The believing community in its various sectarian expressions had recourse to supernatural forces, to the spirit world, to the renewal of esoteric traditions, and sometimes to pre-Christian beliefs and rituals that had been neglected in their deeper dynamics since the coming of Christianity. Even within traditional Christianity there was an intensification of the faith experience, an effort to activate supernatural forces with special powers of intervention in the phenomenal world now viewed as threatening to the human community. The sense of human depravity increased. The need for an outpouring of influences from the higher numinous world was intensified. Faith dominated the religious experience. Redemption mystique became the overwhelming form of Christian experience.

Such excessive emphasis on redemption, to the neglect of the revelatory import of the natural world, had from the beginning been one of the possibilities in Christian development. The creed itself is overbalanced in favor of redemption. Thus the integrity of the Christian story is affected. Creation becomes increasingly less important. This response, with its emphasis on redemptive spirituality, continued through the religious upheavals of the sixteenth century and on through the Puritanism and Jansenism of the seventeenth century. This attitude was further strengthened by the shock of the Enlightenment and Revolution periods of the eighteenth and nineteenth centuries.

The American version of the ancient Christian story has functioned well in its institutional efficiency and in its moral efficacy, but it is no longer the story of the earth. Nor is it the integral story of the human community. It is a sectarian story. At its center there is an intensive preoccupation with the personality of the Savior, with the interior spiritual life of the faithful, and with the salvific community. The difficulty is that we came to accept this situation as the normal, even the desirable, thing.

The other response to the Black Death was the reaction that led eventually to the scientific secular community of our times. That reaction sought to remedy earthly terror not by supernatural or religious powers, but by understanding and controlling the earth process. Although those working in that trend were at first committed to the esoteric wisdom traditions and to Platonic idealism, they did emphasize the need for empirical examination of the phenomenal world and its expression in quantitative terms. Scientific inquiry became the controlling human preoccupation, pushed by obscure forces in the unconscious depths of Western culture. The telescope and microscope were invented. Calculus, the supreme instrument of modern science, was discovered. A scientific priesthood came to govern the thought life of our society. We looked at the earth in its physical reality and projected new theories of how it functioned. The celestial bodies were scrutinized more intently, the phenomenon of light was examined, new ways of understanding energy evolved. New sciences emerged. The *Novum Organum* of Francis Bacon appeared in 1620, the *Principia* of Isaac Newton in 1687, the *Scienza Nuova* of Giambattista Vico in 1725.

All of these led to an awareness that the human mind was advancing. This in turn led to the Enlightenment period of the eighteenth century and to the sense of absolute progress of the human mind as expressed by Condorcet in his 1793 volume entitled *Historical Survey of the Progress of the Human Mind*. In the nineteenth century the doctrines of social development appear with Fourier, Saint-Simon, and August Comte. Karl Marx brought this movement to its most realistic expression in his 1848 *Manifesto*.

While these changes in the mode of human perception and of social structure were taking place, evidence was appearing in the realms of geology and paleontology indicating that there was a time sequence in the very formation of the earth and of all lifeforms upon the earth. The earth was not the eternal, fixed, abiding reality that it had been thought to be. It suddenly dawned upon Western consciousness that earlier lifeforms were of a simpler nature than later lifeforms, that the later forms were derived from the earlier forms. The complex of life manifestations had not existed from the beginning by some external divine creative act setting all things in their place. The earth in all its parts, especially in its lifeforms, was in a state of continuing transformation.

Discovery of this life sequence, with an explanation of how it came about, found expression in Darwin's *Origin of Species* in 1859. After Darwin, the physicists in their study of light and radiation came almost simultaneously to an understanding of the infra-atomic world and the entire galactic system. Insight into both the microphase and macrophase of the phenomenal world was obtained, and the great unity of the universe became apparent both in its spatial expansion and its time sequence.

Just at that moment, however, a sudden shift in the mode of consciousness took place. The scientists suddenly became aware that the opaqueness of matter had dissolved. Science was ultimately not the objective grasping of some reality extrinsic to ourselves. It was rather a moment of subjective communion in which the human was seen as that being in whom the universe in its evolutionary dimension became conscious of itself.

Thus a new creation story had evolved in the secular scientific community, equivalent in our times to the creation stories of antiquity. This creation story differs from the traditional Eurasian creation stories much more than those traditional stories differ one from another. This new creation story seems destined to become the universal story taught to every child who receives formal education in its modern form anywhere in the world.

The redemptive believing community, first dazzled by this new vision of developmental time, then frustrated by an inability to cope with the new data, lapsed unenthusiastically into its traditional attitudes. In recent centuries, indeed, the believing community has not been concerned with any cosmology, ancient or modern, for the believing community has its real values concentrated in the Savior, the human person, the believing church, and a post-earthly paradisal beatitude.

There is, however, a surviving cosmology in which the redemption story takes place and which to some extent still plays a role in the Christian story. According to this story the cosmos, and every being in the cosmos, reflects the divine exemplar considered by Plato as the Agathon, the Good; by Plotinus as the One; by the Christian as God. All things are beautiful by this beauty. The supremely beautiful is the integrity and harmony of the total cosmic order, as Saint Thomas insists upon repeatedly.

The human mind ascends to the contemplation of the divine by rising through the various grades of being, from the physical forms of existence in the earth, with its mountains and seas, to the various forms of living things, and so to the human mode of consciousness, then to the soul, and from the inner life of the soul to God. This sequence, portrayed first in the *Symposium* of Plato, is presented in all its sublime qualities in the soliloquy of Augustine as he meditated with his mother by the window just prior to her death. So Bonaventure could write on the reduction of all the arts and sciences to theology, for all eventually depend upon the divine reference. So, too, the journey of Dante through the various spheres of reality up to the divine vision in itself. Initiation into the basic human and Christian values was initiation into this cosmology. Christian spirituality was built up in this manner. The mysteries of Christianity were integral with this cosmology.

The difficulty with this cosmology is that it presents the world simply as an ordered complex of beings that are ontologically related as an image of the divine. It does not present the world as a continuing process of emergence in which there is an inner organic bond of descent of each reality from an earlier reality.

Yet in their functional roles neither this traditional cosmology nor the new scientific cosmology has been of serious religious concern because of the shift in the Western religious tradition from a dominant creation mystique to a dominant redemption mystique. This Christian redemptive mystique is little concerned with the natural world. The essential thing is redemption out of the world through a personal savior relationship that transcends all such concerns. Even the earlier mystical experiences of ascending to the divine through the realms of created perfection are diminished.

Presently this excessive redemptive emphasis is played out. It cannot effectively dynamize activity in time because it is an inadequate story of time. The redemption story has grown apart not only from the historical story, but also from the earth story. Consequently an isolated spiritual power has eventuated that is being victimized by entropy.

If this is the impasse of the believing redemption community of America, the impasse of the secular scientific community, committed to a developmental universe, is the commitment to the realm of the physical to the exclusion of the spiritual. This has been the tough, the realistic, position. The Darwinian principle of natural selection involves no psychic or conscious purpose, but is instead a struggle for earthly survival that gives to the world its variety of form and function. Because this story presents the universe as a random sequence of physical and biological interactions with no inherent meaning, the society supported by this vision has no adequate way of identifying any spiritual or moral values.

We must not think that these two communities

have no regard for each other. Extensive courtesies are extended; cooperation is offered. Persons in the scientific professions as well as in modern industrial and commercial pursuits have extensive regard for the religious dimension of life. Many are themselves religious personalities. Those in the religious community have their own esteem for scientific, technological, and commercial activities. Training in the professions takes place in religious schools and even dominates the curriculum. So what's the fuss about? The answer is that surface agreement is not depth communion or the basis of sound cosmic-earth-human values. The antagonisms are deeper than they appear. An integral story has not emerged, and no community can exist without a unifying story. This is precisely why the communication between these two is so unsatisfying. No sustaining values have emerged. Our social problems are not resolved. The earth continues to disintegrate under the plundering assault of humans.

Both traditions are trivialized. The human venture remains stuck in its impasse. Children who begin their earth studies or life studies do not experience any numinous aspect of these subjects. The excitement of existence is diminished. If this fascination, this entrancement, with life is not evoked, the children will not have the psychic energies needed to sustain the sorrows inherent in the human condition. They might never discover their true place in the vast world of time and space. Teaching children about the natural world should be treated as one of the most important events in their lives. Children need a story that will bring personal meaning together with the grandeur and meaning of the universe. The secular school as presently constituted cannot provide the mystique that should be associated with this story. Nor can the religious-oriented school that has only superficially adopted this new story of the universe evoke this experience in the child.

The tragedy of this situation is that schooling now fulfills a role in our society that is similar to the role of initiation ceremonies in earlier tribal societies. In those societies the essential mystery communicated to the youthful initiates was the story of the universe in its awesome and numinous aspects. The capacity for communing with and absorbing into their own beings these deeper powers of the natural world was bestowed on them. The pathos in our own situation is that our secular society does not see the numinous quality or the deeper psychic powers associated with its own story, while the religious society rejects the story because it is presented only in its physical aspect. The remedy for this is to establish a deeper understanding of the spiritual dynamics of the universe as revealed through our own empirical insight into the mysteries of its functioning.

In this late twentieth century that can now be done with a clarity never before available to us. Empirical inquiry into the universe reveals that from its beginning in the galactic system to its earthly expression in human consciousness the universe carries within itself a psychic-spiritual as well as a physical-material dimension. Otherwise human consciousness emerges out of nowhere. The human is seen as an addendum or an intrusion and thus finds no real place in the story of the universe. In reality the human activates the most profound dimension of the universe itself, its capacity to reflect on and celebrate itself in conscious self-awareness.

So far, however, spiritually oriented personalities have been pleased because the mechanistic orientation of the scientific world enables them to assume an aloof spiritual attitude that disdains any concern for the natural world. Scientists, on the other hand, are pleased since that attitude leaves them free to structure their world of quantitative measurements without the problem of spiritual values associated with human consciousness. Thus both scientists and believers remain disengaged from any profound understanding of the earth process itself. To remedy this situation, we need simply to reflect on the story itself.

The story of the universe is the story of the emergence of a galactic system in which each new level of expression emerges through the urgency of self-transcendence. Hydrogen in the presence of some millions of degrees of heat emerges into helium. After the stars take shape as oceans of fire in the heavens, they go through a sequence of transformations. Some eventually explode into the stardust out of which the solar system and the earth take shape. Earth gives unique expresson of itself in its rock and crystalline structures and in the variety and splendor of living forms, until humans appear as the moment in which the unfolding universe becomes conscious of itself. The human emerges not only as an earthling, but also as a worldling. We bear the universe in our beings as the universe bears us in its being. The two have a total presence to each other and to that deeper mystery out of which both the universe and ourselves have emerged.

If this integral vision is something new both to the scientist and to the believer, both are gradually becoming aware of this view of the real and its human meaning. It might be considered a new revelatory experience. Because we are moving into a new mythic age, it is little wonder that a kind of mutation is taking place in the entire earth-human order. A new paradigm of what it is to be human emerges. This is what is so exciting, yet so painful and so disrupting. One aspect of this change involves the shift in earth-human relations, for we now in large measure determine the earth process that once determined us. In a more integral way we could say that the earth that controlled itself directly in the former period now to an extensive degree controls itself through us.

In this new context the question appears as to where the values are, how they are determined, how they are transmitted. Whereas formerly values consisted in the perfection of the earthly image reflecting an external Logos in a world of fixed natures, values are now determined by the human sensitivity in responding to the creative urgencies of a developing world. The scientist in the depths of the unconscious is drawn by the mystical attraction of communion with the emerging creative process. This would not be possible unless it were a call of subject to subject, if it were not an effort at total self-realization on the part of the scientists. As scientists, their taste for the real is what gives to their work its admirable quality.

Their wish is to experience the real in its tangible, opaque, material aspect and to respond to that by establishing an interaction with the world that will advance the total process. If the demand for objectivity and the quantitative aspect of the real has led scientists to neglect subjectivity and the qualitative aspect of the real, this has been until now a condition for fulfilling their historical task. The most notable single development within science in recent years, however, has been a growing awareness of the integral physical-psychic dimension of reality.

The believing redemption community is awakening only slowly to this new context of understanding. There is a fear, a distrust, even a profound aversion, to the natural world and all its processes. It would be difficult to find a theological seminary in this country that has an adequate program on creation as it is experienced in these times. The theological curriculum is dominated by a long list of courses on redemption and how it functions in aiding humans to transcend the world, all based on biblical texts. Such a situation cannot long endure, however, since a new sense of the earth and its revelatory import is arising in the believing community. The earth will not be ignored, nor will it long endure being despised, neglected, or mistreated. The dynamics of creation are demanding attention once more in a form unknown for centuries to the orthodox Christian.

It is clear that the primordial intention of the universe is to produce variety in all things, from atomic structures to the living world of plant and animal forms, to the appearance of humans, where individuals differ from one another more extensively than in any other realm of known reality. This difference can be seen not only in individuals, but also in social structures and in historical periods of our development. But here, also, the difficulty in the human order, for there is no absolute model for the individual. Personal realization involves a unique creative effort in response to all those interior and exterior forces that enter into individual life. So, too, with each historical age and each cultural form, there is need to create a reality for which, again, there is no adequate model. This is precisely the American difficulty, a difficulty for which there is no complete answer, but only a striving toward. At each moment we must simply be what we are, opening onto a larger life.

Interior articulation of its own reality is the immediate responsibility of every being. Every being has its own interior, its self, its mystery, its numinous aspect. To deprive any being of this sacred quality is to disrupt the larger order of the universe. Reverence will be total or it will not be at all. The universe does not come to us in pieces any more than a human individual stands before us with some part of its being. Preservation of this feeling for reality in its depths has been considerably upset in these past two centuries of scientific analysis and technological manipulation of the earth and its energies. During this period, the human mind lived in the narrowest bonds that it has ever experienced. The vast mythic, visionary, symbolic world with its all-pervasive numinous qualities was lost. Because of this loss, we made our terrifying assault upon the earth with an irrationality that is stunning in enormity, while we were being assured that this was the way to a better, more humane, more reasonable world.

Such treatment of the external physical world, deprived of its subjectivity, could not long avoid also encompassing the human. Thus we have the most vast paradox of all—ourselves as free, intelligent, numinous beings negating those very interior qualities by our own objective reasoning processes and subserving our own rationalizations. Yet, finally, a reversal has begun, and the reality and value of the interior subjective numinous aspect of the entire cosmic order is being appreciated as the basic condition in which the story makes any sense at all.

Here we come to the further realization that the universe is coherent within itself throughout the total extent of space and the entire sequence of its time development. This web of relationships throughout the universe is what first impinges on our waking consciousness. It is this deepening association within the universe that enables life to emerge into being. The living form is more individuated, with greater subjectivity and more intensive identity within itself and with its environment. All these factors are multiplied on a new scale of magnitude in the realm of consciousness. There a supreme mode of communion exists within the individual, with the human community, within the earth-human complex. Increased capacity for personal identity is inseparable from this capacity for mutual presence. Together this distance and this intimacy establish the basic norms of being, of life, of value. It is the mission of our present and all future generations to develop this capacity for mutual presence on new and more comprehensive levels.

In transmitting values through the sequence of generations, we no longer have the initiation techniques whereby the vision and values of earlier generations were transmitted to succeeding generations. Yet there is an abiding need to assist succeeding generations to fulfill their proper role in the ongoing adventure of the earth process. In the human realm education must supply what instinct supplies in the prehuman realm. There is need for a program to aid the young to identify themselves in the comprehensive dimensions of space and time. This was easier in the world of the *Timaeus,* where the earth was seen as an image of the eternal Logos. In such a world Saint Thomas could compose his masterful presentation of Christian thought, and the place and role of the human within that context. This could then be summarized in catechetical form and taught to succeeding generations.

Now a new way of understanding values is required. We are returning to a more traditional context of story as our source of understanding and value. It is somewhat fascinating to realize that the final achievement of our scientific inquiry into the structure and functioning of the universe as evolutionary process is much closer to the narrative mode of explanation given in the Bible than it is to the later, more philosophical mode of Christian explanation provided in our theologies.

It is of utmost importance that succeeding generations become aware of the larger story outlined here and the numinous, sacred values that have been present in an expanding sequence over this entire time of the world's existence. Within this context all our human affairs—all professions, occupations, and activities—have their meaning precisely insofar as they enhance this emerging world of subjective intercommunion within the total range of reality. Within this context the scientific community and the religious community have a common basis. The limitations of the redemption rhetoric and the scientific rhetoric can be seen, and a new, more integral language of being and value can emerge.

Within this story a structure of knowledge can be established, with its human significance, from the physics of the universe and its chemistry through geology and biology to economics and commerce and so to all those studies whereby we fulfill our role in the earth process. There is no way of guiding the course of human affairs through the perilous course of the future except by discovering our role in this larger evolutionary process. If the way of Western civilization and Western religion was once the way of election and differentiation from others and from the earth, the way now is the way of intimate communion wth the larger human community and with the universe itself.

Here we might observe that the basic mood of the

future might well be one of confidence in the continuing revelation that takes place in and through the earth. If the dynamics of the universe from the beginning shaped the course of the heavens, lighted the sun, and formed the earth, if this same dynamism brought forth the continents and seas and atmosphere, if it awakened life in the primordial cell and then brought into being the unnumbered variety of living beings, and finally brought us into being and guided us safely through the turbulent centuries, there is reason to believe that this same guiding process is precisely what has awakened in us our present understanding of ourselves and our relation to this stupendous process. Sensitized to such guidance from the very structure and functioning of the universe, we can have confidence in the future that awaits the human venture.

THE DREAM
OF THE EARTH

.⸱⟡⸱.

IN THIS LATE twentieth century we are somewhat
confused about our human situation. We need
guidance. Our immediate tendency is to seek guidance from our cultural traditions, from what might
be designated as our cultural coding. Yet in this case
our need seems to be for guidance that is beyond what
our cultural traditions are able to give. These traditions, it seems, are themselves a major source of
difficulty. It appears necessary that we go beyond our
cultural coding, to our genetic coding, to ask for
guidance.

We seldom consider going to our genetic coding
for guidance in our cultural development because we
are generally unaware that our genetic coding provides the basic psychic and physical structure of our

being. Our genetic coding determines not only our identity at birth; its guidance continues also in every cell of our bodies throughout the entire course of our existence, a guidance manifested through the spontaneities within us. We need only to listen to what we are being told through the very structure and functioning of our being. We do invent our cultural coding, but the power to do so is itself consequent on the imperatives of our genetic coding.

Beyond our genetic coding, we need to go to the earth, as the source whence we came, and ask for its guidance, for the earth carries the psychic structure as well as the physical form of every living being upon the planet. Our confusion is not only within ourselves; it concerns also our role in the planetary community. Even beyond the earth, we need to go to the universe and inquire concerning the basic issues of reality and value, for, even more than the earth, the universe carries the deep mysteries of our existence within itself.

We cannot discover ourselves without first discovering the universe, the earth, and the imperatives of our own being. Each of these has a creative power and a vision far beyond any rational thought or cultural creation of which we are capable. Nor should we think of these as isolated from our own individual being or from the human community. We have no existence except within the earth and within the universe.

The human is less a being on the earth or in the universe than a dimension of the earth and indeed of the universe itself. The shaping of our human mode of being depends on the support and guidance of this comprehensive order of things. We are an immediate concern of every other being in the universe. Ultimately our guidance on any significant issue must emerge from this comprehensive source.

Nor is this source distant from us. The universe is so immediate to us, is such an intimate presence, that it escapes our notice, yet whatever authenticity exists in our cultural creations is derived from these spontaneities within us, spontaneities that come from an abyss of energy and a capacity for intelligible order of which we have only the faintest glimmer in our conscious awareness.

Our bonding with the larger dimensions of the universe comes about primarily through our genetic coding. It is the determining factor. It provides constant guidance in the organic functioning that takes place in all our sense functions; in our capacity for transforming food into energy; in our thought, imaginative, and emotional life. In a particular manner the genetic coding brings about a healing whenever we sustain any physical injury. Our genetic coding enables us to experience joy and sorrow on appropriate occasions. It provides the ability to speak and think and create. It establishes the context of our relation with the divine. All this is carried out by the spontaneities within us.

Although we must respond critically with these spontaneities to assure their authentic expression, we have ultimately no other source of guidance that possesses such inherent authenticity or which can function so effectively as a norm of reference in our actions. In earlier times these spontaneities were considered as revealing the natural law, the ultimate inner norm of guidance for human conduct, since they are the human phase of those instincts that enable a bird to build its nest, find its food, and discover its migratory route. Ultimately these instincts come from that mysterious source from where the universe itself came into being as articulated entities acting together in some ordered context.

Saint John tells us that in the beginning all things took on their shape through the word. The word was seen as psychic and personal. This was the numinous reality through which all things were made and without which was made nothing that has been made. The word, the self-spoken word, by its own spontaneities brought forth the universe and established itself as the ultimate form of reality and of value. This is in accord with Lao Tzu, the Chinese sage, who tells us that the human models itself on the earth, earth models itself on heaven, heaven models itself on tao, tao models itself on its own spontaneity.

This spontaneity as the guiding force of the universe can be thought of as the mysterious impulse whereby the primordial fireball flared forth in its enormous energy, a fireball that contained in itself all that would ever emerge into being, a fireball that was the present in its primordial form, as the present is the fireball in its explicated form. What enabled the formless energies to emerge into such a fantastic variety of expression in shape, color, scent, feeling, thought, and imagination?

As with any aesthetic work, we attribute it especially to the imaginative capacities of the artist, for only out of imaginative power does any grand creative work take shape. Since imagination functions most freely in dream vision, we tend to associate creativity also with dream experience. The dream comes about precisely through the uninhibited spontaneities of which we are speaking. In this context we might say: In the beginning was the dream. Through the dream all things were made, and without the dream nothing was made that has been made.

While all things share in this dream, as humans we share in this dream in a special manner. This is the entrancement, the magic of the world about us, its mystery, its ineffable quality. What primordial source could, with no model for guidance, imagine such a fantastic world as that in which we live—the shape of the orchid, the coloring of the fish in the sea, the winds and the rain, the variety of sounds that flow over the earth, the resonant croaking of the bullfrogs, the songs of the crickets, and the pure joy of the predawn singing of the mockingbird?

Experience of such a resplendent world activated the creative imagination of Mozart in *The Magic Flute,* of Dante in his *Divine Comedy,* and gave to Shakespeare that range of sensitivity, understanding, and emotion that found expression in his plays. All of these derive from the visionary power that is experienced most profoundly when we are immersed in the depths of our own being and of the cosmic order itself in the dreamworld that unfolds within us in our sleep, or in those visionary moments that seize upon us in our waking hours. There we discover the Platonic forms, the dreams of Brahman, the Hermetic mysteries, the divine ideas of Thomas Aquinas, the infinite worlds of Giordano Bruno, the world soul of the Cambridge Platonists, the self-organizing universe of Ilya Prigogine, the archetypal world of C.G. Jung.

Each of these is enormously attractive, having a certain inner coherence and revealing some aspect of the universe and of the planet Earth that is fascinating to the human mind. They can be understood as facets of a mystery too vast for human comprehension, a mystery with such power that even a fragment of its grandeur can evoke the great human cultural enterprises. In this context we have shaped our languages and lifestyles, our poetry and music, our religious scriptures, our political ideals, our humanistic literature, our life-sustaining economies. Of special importance is the grand sequence of rituals whereby we insert ourselves into the ever-renewing sequence of springtime renewals in nature.

The excitement of life and the sustaining of psychic vigor are evoked by our participation in this magnificent process. Even before we give expression to any intellectual statement about the natural world, we stand in awe at the stars splashed in such prodigal display across the heavens, at the earth in its shaping of the seas and the continents, at the great hydrological cycles that lift such vast quantities of water up from the seas and rain them down over the land to nourish the meadows and the forests and to refresh the animals as the waters flow down through the valleys and back again to the seas. We marvel, too, at the millionfold sequence of living foms, from the plankton in the sea and the bacteria in the soil to the larger lifeforms that swim through the oceans and grow up from the soil and move over the land.

Much could be said, too, about the human as that being in whom this grand diversity of the universe celebrates itself in conscious self-awareness. While we emerge into being from within the earth process and enable the universe to come to itself in a special mode of psychic intimacy, it is evident that we have also a special power over the universe in its earthly expression. Therein lies the dramatic issue that is being played out in these centuries of human time that succeed to the ages of geological and biological time.

From our vantage point we can sketch out the great story of the universe from its beginning until now. We can recognize the earth as a privileged planet and see the whole as evolving out of some cosmic imaginative process. Any significant thought or speech about the universe finds its expression through such imaginative powers. Even our scientific terms have a highly mythic content—such words as *energy, life, matter, form, universe, gravitation, evolution*.

Even such terms as *atom, nucleus, electron, molecule, cell, organism.* Each of these terms spills over into metaphor and mystery as soon as it is taken seriously.

As regards the origin and shaping forces in the universe, the geneticist Theodosius Dobzhansky considers that the universe in its emergence is neither determined nor random, but creative. This word *creative* is among the most mysterious words in any language. As with our words generally, this term, too, has been trivialized. Its numinous and its magic qualities have been diminished, also its visionary quality. We have substituted our real world of facts and figures for our visionary world.

We must reflect, however, on what we have gained in this substitution and what we have lost. We have lost our principal means of entering into the primordial directive and sustaining forces of the universe. We have in a very special manner lost our presence to the life-sustaining forces of the earth. Whatever our gains in terms of scientific advances or in our industrial economy, neither of these is very helpful in establishing an integral presence to the more profound depths of our own being or into the more powerful forces shaping both the universe and the planet on which we live.

Inherent in the human situation is the problem of

keeping our cultural expression integrally related to our genetic endowment. Through our genetic endowment we maintain our intimate presence to the functioning of the earth community and to the emergent processes of the universe itself. This problem of properly relating cultural coding to the imperatives of our genetic coding is the central, the immediate, problem, a problem that does not exist, or exists only in a minimal degree, with other species.

The human, we must understand, is genetically coded toward a further transgenetic cultural coding whereby we invent ourselves in the human expression of our being. While this capacity for self-formation is a high privilege, it is also a significant responsibility, since the powers we possess also give us extensive control over a wide range of earthly affairs. This cultural coding, once it is articulated as the functioning norm of a human community, is handed on by educational processes through parental care from the moment of birth. After birth a long educational process takes place that requires a family context with the assistance of a larger human community.

Because this cultural coding is freely determined, it finds expression in a wide diversity of forms throughout the human community. Once established as the normative reference of reality and value within the community, this cultural coding is carried on and expressed in the language and in the symbols that are learned quite early in life. The relation between our cultural coding and our genetic coding is evident in our use of language. We are genetically coded to speak, but the specific manner of our speech is our own invention. So, too, with the genetic imperative that we live in society. How we shape our social functioning is again our own invention. So it is with the rituals whereby we insert ourselves into the ever-renewing processes of the natural world and establish our world of meaning, our sense of reality and value.

All these are means whereby we articulate our special mode of being and fulfill our role in the universal order of things, all in response to the spontaneities that emerge from our genetic coding; ultimately, of course, they emerge from the larger community of life, from the integral functioning of the planet Earth, from the comprehensive functioning of the universal order of things, and from that numinous source from which all things receive their being, their energy, and their inherent grandeur.

We need to remember that this process whereby we invent ourselves in these cultural modes is guided by visionary experiences that come to us in some transrational process from the inner shaping tendencies that we carry within us, often in revelatory dream experience. Such dream experiences are so universal and so important in the psychic life of the individual and of the community that techniques of dreaming are taught in some societies.

In some societies, also, the early morning gatherings are used for interpretation of the dream experiences of the previous night. This was the case with the Algonquin peoples of this continent when they were first observed by European missionaries. In some of the early reports, dreams were seen as so important that the religion of the Indians was identified as a religion of dreams.

Dreams were the main instrument of guidance in their daily activities as well as in the larger interpretation of life, for if our daytime experience is needed for awakening to the phenomenal world, our nighttime experience is needed for communion with those numinous powers from which the daylight forms themselves come into being. The great phases of cultural development are consistently attributed to such experiences.

Over time this cultural coding of human communities has been articulated in its early Paleolithic tribal phase, its Neolithic village phase, then its classical civilizational phase, when the more populous centers arose with their more spacious architecture, their written literatures, their more elaborate religious, political, and economic establishments.

These achievements, which are sometimes designated as the full realization of the human mode of being, have a certain tendency to disintegrate in the manner that we are presently experiencing. Giambattista Vico, the eighteenth-century Neopolitan interpreter of human history, considered that the eighteenth century was the period when a second barbarism, a barbarism of refinement, erupted in the civilizational enterprise. A new descent into a more primitive state must then come about, a reimmersion in the natural forces out of which our cultural achievements came about originally. The forces of primitive imagination once again were required to renew the cultural integrity. A new contact with genetic coding was mandated.

Even while we indicate the role that is played by the dream vision in the cultural development of the human, we must also realize that the dream vision can be destructive as well as creative. It is a dangerous process if we are not fully sensitized to what our genetic coding is telling us. It has become especially dangerous in Western civilization when our cultural coding has set itself deliberately against our genetic coding and the instinctive tendencies of our genetic endowment are systematically negated. Such is the origin of our present situation.

Our secular, rational, industrial society, with its amazing scientific insight and technological skills, has established the first radically anthropocentric society and has thereby broken the primary law of the universe, the law of the integrity of the universe, the law that every component member of the universe should be integral with every other member of the universe and that the primary norm of reality and of value is the universe community itself in its various forms of expression, especially as realized on the planet Earth.

This new industrial coding, which arose first in Western society, has now been spread throughout the earth. Few peoples anywhere have escaped its influence. The relation of the human community to its genetic coding and to the entire functioning of the natural world is decisively altered. A profound shift in meaning is given to the entire evolutionary process.

The immediate advantages of this new way of life for its prime beneficiaries have been evident throughout these past two centuries. But, now, suddenly we begin to experience disaster on a scale never before thought possible. For a long while we looked back at prior times and the mythic accounts of how the world came into being, the sequence of transformations and the role of the human in the larger processes of nature; we looked back at these stories, at the revelatory dreams of these earlier peoples, at their sense of numinous energies governing the phenomenal world, at their efforts to establish contact with these powers through strange shamanic performances or through more-programmed initiatory and sacrificial rituals; we looked back at all this with a certain disdain for these dark ages, although with a restrained envy of the visions recorded in their sacred literature, of their heroic experiences, and often of an artistic grandeur that we could not match.

We were the sane, the rational, the dreamless people, the chosen people of destiny. We had found the opening to a more just society, a more reasoning intellectual life. Above all we had the power to re-engineer the planet with our energy systems, our dams and irrigation projects, our great cities. We could clear the forests, drain the marshes, construct our railways and highways, all to the detriment of the other living forms of earth, to the elimination of needed habitat, to the obstruction of migration paths, to the cutting off of access to waterways. We could subdue the wilderness, domesticate the planet.

We were finally free from the tyranny of nature. Nature was now our servant, delivering up to us its energies, altering its biological rhythms in accord with our mechanical contrivances.

The human condition could be overcome by our entrepreneurial skills. Nuclear energy would give us limitless power. Through genetic engineering we could turn chickens into ever more effective egg-laying machines, cows into milk-making machines, steers into meat-making contrivances, all according to human preference, not according to the inner spontaneities of these living beings as determined by their genetic coding, a coding shaped through some billions of years of experiment and natural selection.

Ever-heightened consumption was the way to ultimate human fulfillment. Every earthly being was reduced from its status as a sacred reality to that of being a "natural resource," available for human use for whatever trivial purposes humans might invent. It would take a while to describe what has been happening in all our professions and institutions in this period of assumed cultural progress.

This magical word *progress!* Although long ago discredited as an illusory belief, we still hear the word spoken with a kind of religious reverence, even as a final norm of reference in any consideration of reality and value. Loren Eiseley has written a description of our present relationship with nature: "We have reentered nature, not like a Greek shepherd on a hillside hearing joyfully the returning pipes of Pan, but rather as an evil and precocious animal who slinks home in the night with a few stolen powers. The serenity of the gods is not disturbed. They know on whose head the final lightning will fall."

Suddenly we awaken to the devastation that has resulted from the entire modern process. A thousand pages would be needed to recount what has happened. It can best be summarized by the title of Rachel Carson's book, *Silent Spring,* a title taken from Keats: "The sedge is withered from the lake/and no birds sing." The book itself is dedicated to Albert Schweitzer, who tells us: "Man has lost the capacity to foresee and to forestall. He will end by destroying the earth."

This is a bitter moment, not simply for the human, but for the earth itself. The biblical slaughter of the innocents is only a faint foreshadowing of the slaughter of the innocents taking place in these times, when the innocents are not simply individuals capable of replacement within their species, but the slaughter of species themselves, irreversibly, eternally.

It is a bitter moment especially because our hopes

were so high, our arrogance unrestrained even by simple modesty. It is a bitter moment, also, because the origins of our actions go so deep into our spiritual and cultural traditions, fostering a sense that we are the measure of all things. Our sense of endless progress emerges from the millennial expectations of our scriptures. From the prophetic period onward our scriptures speak to us of a period when the human condition would be surmounted, when justice would reign, when the fruits of the earth would be available in lavish abundance. All this fostered a profound resentment against our human condition.

We somehow did not belong to the community of earth. We were not an integral component of the natural world. Our destiny was not here. We deserved a better world, although we had not even begun to appreciate the beauty and grandeur of this world or the full measure of its entrancing qualities.

What we seem unwilling or unable to recognize is that our entire modern world is itself inspired not by any rational process, but by a distorted dream experience, perhaps by the most powerful dream that has ever taken possession of human imagination. Our sense of progress, our entire technological society, however rational in its functioning, is a pure dream vision in its origin and in its objectives. This dream vision of the coming Day of the Lord, as mentioned by the prophets, was taken up by Daniel in his interpretation of the apocalyptic dream of Nebuchadnezzar. Although this entrancing vision of the universe was originally presented as the spiritual triumph of the divine kingdom, it was later described by John the Evangelist as a blissful period beyond the human condition, to be experienced within the historical order prior to the ultimate transference of the kingdom to its celestial setting.

The story of this dream vision and the manner of its transformation into the vision of progress has become the central story of the human community, even of the earth process itself. René Dubos caught the significance of our more recent commitment to progress in the title of his book *The Dreams of Reason*. That very rational process that we exalt as the only true way to understanding is by a certain irony discovered to be itself a mythic, imaginative dream experience.

The difficulty of our times is our inability to awaken out of this cultural pathology. Thousands of articles have been written and a long list of books could be compiled concerning this commitment to progress and to the sense of unlimited growth that it evokes. Yet its control over the human venture remains more vigorous than ever. Whatever the validity of the original vision of an unfolding spiritual progress, this vision has proved too much for humans to manage in any disciplined way.

The difficulty is that this dream of a millennial transformation to be achieved by science and technology under the direction of the modern corporation is thought of as the singular reality controlling all things and giving meaning to the whole of history. This vision alone makes life worthwhile. That is why the millennial vision is so important to the advertising industry, with its projection of a paradise that can be obtained through product consumption, any product.

When the absurdity of progress through exponential growth was indicated a few years ago in a work entitled *The Limits to Growth,* a general outcry could be heard across the country. That outcry was more than a justified criticism of the specific data or the time scale of future events. It was resentment against the indication that the dynamism of our consumer society was the supreme pathology of all history.

Use of the term *supreme pathology* can be justified by the observation that the change that is taking place in the present is not simply another historical transition or another cultural transformation. Its order of magnitude is immensely more significant in its nature and in its consequences. We are indeed closing down the major life systems of the planet.

We are acting on a geological and biological order of magnitude. We are changing the chemistry of the planet. We are altering the great hydrological cycles. We are weakening the ozone layer that shields us from cosmic rays. We are saturating the air, the water, and the soil with toxic substances so that we can never bring them back to their original purity. We are upsetting the entire earth system that has, over some billions of years and through an endless sequence of experiments, produced such a magnificent array of living forms, forms capable of seasonal self-renewal over an indefinite period of time.

That the changes taking place are of this order of magnitude can be supported by reference to a conference held in September 1986 in Washington, D.C., a conference on the future of living species sponsored by the National Academy of Sciences and the Smithsonian Institution. There our foremost biologists expressed their forebodings concerning the future.

E. O. Wilson from Harvard indicated that we are losing ten thousand species a year and that this rate of loss is increasing. Norman Myers, a specialist in the rain forests and vegetation of the world, said that the "impending extinction spasm" is likely to produce the "greatest single setback to life's abundance and diversity since the first flickerings of life almost four billion years ago." Other speakers agreed that our present extinction of living forms is, in its enormity, paralleled only by the great geological and climatic upheavals that changed the earth in the distant past.

Paul Ehrlich, who has studied the questions of extinction for more than twenty years, made some of the most startling statements. He observed that "humanity will bring upon itself consequences depressingly similar to those expected from a nuclear winter," and he expects them to be accompanied by the famine and epidemic disease generally associated with the concept of nuclear winter.

Both Wilson and Ehrlich were concerned with questions of human conduct in dealing with such devastation. Wilson proposed that in the end "I suspect it will all come down to a decision of ethics, how we value the natural world in which we have evolved and now—increasingly—how we regard our situation as individuals." Ehrlich considers that to look to technology for a solution "would be a lethal mistake." His final suggestion was that "scientific analysis points, curiously, toward the need for a quasi-religious transformation of contemporary cultures."

My own suggestion is that we must go far beyond any transformation of contemporary culture. We must go back to the genetic imperative from which human cultures emerge originally and from which they can never be separated without losing their integrity and their survival capacity. None of our existing cultures can deal with this situation out of its own resources. We must invent, or reinvent, a sustainable human culture by a descent into our prerational, our instinctive, resources. Our cultural resources have lost their integrity. They cannot be trusted. What is needed is not transcendence but "inscendence," not the brain but the gene.

The assumption about traditional cultural codings is that they will foster rather than suppress or extinguish those more profound imperatives that govern the universe in its physical structures, its chemical composition, and its biological forms, as well as in its human expression. Indeed the species coding of the human carries within itself all those deeper spontaneities that guide the authentic developments of our cultural codings.

The genetic coding that gives to the human its species identity is integral with this larger complex of codings whereby the universe exists, whereby the earth system remains coherent within itself and capable of continuing the evolutionary process. To remain viable a species must establish a niche for itself that is beneficial both for itself and for the surrounding community. The difficulty with this proposal is that our genetic endowment is considered to be a mere physical determination of our being, not also our richest psychic endowment, our guiding and inspiring force, especially when the cultural process has entered into a destructive pathology.

This pathology is manifest in the arrogance with which we reject our role as an integral member of the earth community in favor of a radical anthropocentric life attitude. The critical moment of rejection of our role as an integral member of the earth community was reached in the work of Thomas Huxley in his famous Romanes lecture, "Evolution and Ethics," given in 1893. Human social progress he considered as "a checking of the cosmic process at every step and the substitution for it of another, which may be called the ethical process. . . ."

Sigmund Freud wrote even more strongly to this effect in his essay "Civilization and Its Discontents": "Against the dreaded external world one can only defend oneself by some kind of turning away from it, if one intends to solve the task by oneself. There is, indeed, another and better path: that of becoming a member of the human community, and, with the help of a technique guided by science, going over to the attack against nature and subjecting her to the human will."

Both Huxley and Freud saw the human as essentially alien to the larger community of creatures. The basic need was to subject the natural world to the human lest the human become subjected to and possibly destroyed by the natural world. In this context it is easy to understand the attitude that other earthly beings are instruments to be used or resources to be exploited for human benefit. We are too good for the natural world. In ourselves the natural world goes beyond itself into a new and more sublime form of grandeur. Neither Huxley nor Freud had any idea of the disastrous consequences of such an attitude on the integral functioning of the earth or on our human destiny.

Those consequences are now becoming manifest. The day of reckoning has come. In this disintegrating phase of our industrial society, we now see ourselves not as the splendor of creation, but as the most pernicious mode of earthly being. We are the termination, not the fulfillment of the earth process. If there were a parliament of creatures, its first decision might well be to vote the humans out of the community, too deadly a presence to tolerate any further. We are the affliction of the world, its demonic presence. We are the violation of earth's most sacred aspects.

The anthropocentrism from which this violation proceeds is ultimately not an invention of the nineteenth century. Nor is it due simply to the secular scholars of this period. It is enshrined both in our humanistic learning and in our religious and spiritual teachings. The present situation is so extreme that we need to get beyond our existing cultural formation, back to the primary tendencies of our nature itself, as expressed in the spontaneities of our being.

Yet it is not easy for us to move beyond those basic humanistic ideals that have directed our cultural traditions over the past millennia. These anthropocentric traditions have determined our language, our intellectual insights, our educational programs, our spiritual ideals, our imaginative power, our emotional sensitivities. All these can now be seen not only as inadequate, but also as distorted and as the origin of the deteriorating influence that we have on the life systems of the earth.

Our traditional languages express most clearly the anthropocentrism from which our difficulties have emerged. Our imagination is filled with images that sustain the present direction of our culture. Our spiritual values are disorientating with their insistence on the flawed nature of the existing order of things and the need for relief by escape from the earth rather than on a greater intimacy with the earth. Constantly we assert the value of the human over the merely resource values of the natural world. Our legal system fosters a sense of the human as having rights over the rights of natural beings. Our commerce, industry, and economics are based on the devastation of the earth. Disengagement from such basic life commitments requires a certain daring.

In order to get a sense of just how difficult it is to change basic commitments, we might recall the story of the *Titanic* on her maiden voyage. Abundant evidence indicated that icebergs were ahead. Nevertheless, the course was set, and no one wished to alter the direction. Confidence in the survival capacities of the ship was unbounded, and there were already a multitude of other concerns related to carrying out the simply normal routine of the voyage. I relate the story of the *Titanic* here as a kind of parable, since even in dire situations we often do not have the energy required to alter our way of acting on the scale that is required. For us there is still time to change course, to move away from our plundering economy to a more sustainable ecological economy.

We cannot obliterate the continuities of history. Nor can we move into the future without guidance from the more valid elements of our existing cultural forms, yet we must reach far back into the genetic foundations of our cultural formation for a healing and a restructuring at the most basic level. This is particularly true now, since the anthropogenic shock that is overwhelming the earth is of an order of magnitude beyond anything previously known in human historical or cultural development. As we have indicated, only those geological and biological changes of the past that have taken hundreds of millions of years for their accomplishment can be referred to as having any comparable order of magnitude.

The new cultural coding that we need must emerge from the source of all such codings, from revelatory vision that comes to us in those special psychic moments, or conditions, that we describe as "dream." We are, of course, using this term not only as regards the psychic processes that take place when we are physically asleep, but also to indicate an intuitive, nonrational process that occurs when we awaken to the numinous powers ever present in the phenomenal world about us, powers that possess us in our high creative moments. Poets and artists continually invoke these spirit powers, which function less through words than through symbolic forms.

In moments of confusion such as the present, we are not left simply to our own rational contrivances. We are supported by the ultimate powers of the universe as they make themselves present to us through the spontaneities within our own beings. We need only become sensitized to these spontaneities, not with a naive simplicity, but with critical appreciation. This intimacy with our genetic endowment, and through this endowment with the larger cosmic process, is not primarily the role of the philosopher, priest, prophet, or professor. It is the role of the shamanic personality, a type that is emerging once again in our society.

More than any other of the human types concerned with the sacred, the shamanic personality journeys into the far regions of the cosmic mystery and brings back the vision and the power needed by the human community at the most elementary level. The shamanic personality speaks and best understands the language of the creatures of the earth. Not only is the shamanic type emerging in our society, but also the shamanic dimension of the psyche itself. In periods of significant cultural creativity, this aspect of the psyche takes on a pervasive role throughout the society and shows up in all the basic institutions and professions. The great scientists do their best work through this dimension of the psyche.

This shamanic insight is especially important just now when history is being made not primarily within nations or between nations, but between humans and the earth, with all its living creatures. In this context all our professions and institutions must be judged primarily by the extent to which they foster this mutually enhancing human-earth relationship.

If the supreme disaster in the comprehensive story of the earth is our present closing down of the major life systems of the planet, then the supreme need of our times is to bring about a healing of the earth through this mutually enhancing human presence to the earth community. To achieve this mode of pressure, a new type of sensitivity is needed, a sensitivity that is something more than romantic attachment to some of the more brilliant manifestations of the natural world, a sensitivity that comprehends the larger patterns of nature, its severe demands as well as its delightful aspects, and is willing to see the human diminish so that other lifeforms might flourish.

These sensitivities are beginning to emerge throughout the human community in the multitude of activities that can generally be indicated under the general title of ecological movements. Ecology can rightly be considered the supreme subversive science. In responding to the external situation and to the imperatives of our own nature, these ecological movements are threatening all those cultural commitments that have brought about the present devastation of the earth. This rising conflict is beginning to dominate every aspect of the human process.

The ecology movement is answering the countergenetic process that was inaugurated through the industrial revolution. Even deeper than the industrial process, this ecological expression of the genetic imperative is demanding a reorientation of the entire relgious-cultural order. Only recently, however, have the religious, cultural, and educational programs taken the ecological movement seriously. The first and most powerful impact of the ecology movement is felt in a rising resentment toward the economic and industrial processes that are the immediate causes of the difficulty.

Three basic aspects of the ecology movement can be observed: the confrontational, transformational, and creative aspects. Such movements as Greenpeace and Earth First! have a powerful confrontational aspect. The arrogance of the industrial order requires an opposed force of somewhat equal order of commitment. The industrial order is locked into our present cultural coding as well as into our economic institutions. Any radical adjustment appears as a threat to the very existence of the society.

The power of the industrial system is in the pervasive feeling throughout the society that there is no truly human survival or fulfillment except in opposition to the genetic codings of the natural world. Nothing must be left in its natural state. Everything must be sacralized by human use, even though this is momentary and the consequence is an irreversible degradation of the planet.

To the ecologist, survival is possible only within the earth system itself, in the integrity of the earth's functioning within the genetic codings of the biosphere, the physical codings of earth process, and within those comprehensive vast codings that enable the universe to continue as an emergent creative reality. The ultimate coding is expressed in the curvature of the emergent universe. This curve is sufficiently closed to hold all things within an ordered pattern, while it is sufficiently open to enable the creative process itself to continue.

These are the two radical positions—the industrial and the ecological—that confront each other, with survival at stake: survival of the human at an acceptable level of fulfillment on a planet capable of providing the psychic as well as the physical nourishment that is needed. No prior struggle in the course of human affairs ever involved issues at this order of magnitude. If some degree of reconciliation has taken place, it remains minimal in relation to the changes that are needed to restore a viable mode of human presence to the earth.

Yet beginnings are being made. A multitude of institutional changes are being effected. The World Bank is reassessing its activities of the past years: older, destructive programs are being abandoned; new, ecologically viable programs are being introduced. Healing of damaged ecosystems is in process. The Nature Conservancy is managing a large number of natural sites as habitat for a variety of species. The Natural Resources Defense Council is forcing governmental powers to carry out programs to prevent further damage to the earth. A multitude of other organizations are actively engaged in preservation projects.

Foundations are funding projects with a new sense of the urgency, both cultural and economic, of maintaining the integral functioning of the earth. One of the most helpful projects funded in recent years is the

World Resources Institute, which is providing an amazing amount of information on what is happening to the planet. The Worldwatch Institute also is providing a much-needed assessment of our present situation. These are relatively new institutes that must be added to the much older organizations that remain the dominant forces in leading the human community toward a more benign presence upon the earth.

It would take too long to enumerate even the most significant of these movments on a local, national, and international scale. Merely to enumerate the various aspects of our present society that are now actively involved in this renewal of the earth would be difficult. We would have to include the political, legal, economic, and educational activities, the religious and cultural activities, as well as the communications media.

In addition to the confrontational and transformational movements that are presently functioning, we find those even more significant movements that are creating the vision and the functional processes about which the new cultural, economic, social, and legal structures can be developed. Of special mention here might be the bioregional movements. They represent the context for human presence within the natural life communities into which the earth is divided. In the summer of 1987, a North American Green Movement in politics took further shape on a national scale. In the same summer a beginning was made in developing a concern for the future of the earth within the Christian religious traditions.

What I am proposing here is that these prior archetypal forms that guided the course of human affairs are no longer sufficient. Our genetic coding, through the ecological movement and through the bioregional vision, is providing us with a new archetypal world. The universe is revealing itself to us in a special manner just now. Also the planet Earth and the life communities of the earth are speaking to us through the deepest elements of our nature, through our genetic coding.

In relation to the earth, we have been autistic for centuries. Only now have we begun to listen with some attention and with a willingness to respond to the earth's demands that we cease our industrial assault, that we abandon our inner rage against the conditions of our earthly existence, that we renew our human participation in the grand liturgy of the universe.

THE COSMOLOGY
OF PEACE

·~❧~·

THE UNIVERSE, EARTH, LIFE, and consciousness
are all violent processes. The basic terms in cosmology, geology, biology, and anthropology all carry
a heavy charge of tension and violence. Neither the
universe as a whole nor any part of the universe is especially peaceful. As Heraclitus noted, Conflict is the
father of all things.

The elements are born in supernovas. The sun is
lit by gravitational pressures. The air we breathe and
the water we drink come from the volcanic eruptions
of gases from within the earth. The mountains are
formed by the clash of the great continental and oce-
anic segments of the earth's crust.

Life emerges and advances by the struggle of species for more complete life expression. Humans have

made their way amid the harshness of the natural world and have imposed their violence on the natural world. Among themselves humans have experienced unending conflict. An enormous psychic effort has been required to articulate the human mode of being in its full imaginative, emotional, and intellectual qualities, a psychic effort that emerges from and gives expression to that dramatic confrontation of forces that shape the universe. The confrontation may give rise to "the tears of things," as described by Virgil, but its creative function would be difficult to ignore.

Thus while we reflect on the turmoil of the universe in its emergent process, we must also understand the splendor that finds expression amid this sequence of catastrophic events, a splendor that set the context for the emerging human age. This period of the human in its modern form that began perhaps sixty thousand years ago, after some two million years of transitional human types, roughly coincides with the last glacial advance and recession. The recession period is especially important since it was also the Neolithic period of permanent villages, horticulture, and weaving. Humans began establishing patterns of life controlled by intelligence and human decision, which impinged with progressive destructiveness on the patterns of the natural world.

A new violence was released over the planet. But if in prior ages the violence of the natural world was essentially creative in the larger arc of its unfolding, the violence associated with human presence on the planet remains ambivalent in its ultimate consequences. From Heraclitus to Augustine, to Nicholas of Cusa, Hegel, and Marx, to Jung, Teilhard, and Prigogine, creativity has been associated with a disequilibrium, a tension of forces, whether this be in a physical, biological, or consciousness context.

If these tensions often result in destructive moments in the planetary process, these moments have ultimately been transformed in some creative context. As human power over the total process has increased, however, and the spontaneities of nature have been suppressed or extinguished, the proper functioning of the planet has become increasingly dependent on human wisdom and human decision. This dependence began with human intrusion into the natural functioning of the land, that is, with agriculture and the control of water through irrigation. Since then a conquest mentality has been generated coextensive with the civilizational process. The conquest of the earth and its functioning was extended to the conquest of peoples and their lands. The sectioning of the earth and its human inhabitants is a dominant theme in the story of the planet over these many years, until now more than 180 nation-states have established their identity.

These nations exist in an abiding sequence of conflicts that have grown especially virulent in more recent years as our scientific and technological skills have given us increasing control over the enormous powers contained in the physical structures of the earth. The destructive power now available is such that a change of perspective in every phase of earthly existence is required to understand what is happening on the planet and what is happening to the planet. For the first time the planet has become capable of self-destruction in many of its major life systems through human agency, or at least it has become capable of causing a violent and irreversible alteration of its chemical and biological constitution such as has not taken place since the original shaping of the earth occurred.

In our present context, failure in creativity would be an absolute failure. A present failure at this order of magnitude cannot be remedied later by a larger success. In this context a completely new type of creativity is needed. This creativity must have as its primary concern the survival of the earth in its functional integrity. Concern for the well-being of the planet is the one concern that, it is hoped, will bring the nations of the world into an international community. Since the earth functions as an absolute unity, any dysfunctioning of the planet imperils every nation on the planet.

After this concern for the integrity of the earth, the next concern is to see the human itself as an integral member of the earth community, not as some lordly being free to plunder the earth for human utility. The issue of interhuman tensions is secondary to earth-human tensions. If humans will not become functional members of the earth community, how can humans establish functional relationships among themselves? It is not exactly the question of whether the nations can survive each other, nor is it even the question of whether intelligent beings can survive the natural forces of the planet; it is whether the planet can survive the intelligence that it has itself brought forth.

My proposal is that the cosmology of peace is presently the basic issue. The human must be seen in its cosmological role just as the cosmos needs to be seen in its human manifestation. This cosmological context has never been more clear than it is now, when everything depends on a *creative resolution of our present antagonisms*. I refer to a *creative resolution of antagonism* rather than to *peace* in deference to the violent aspects of the cosmological process. Phenomenal existence itself seems to be a violent mode of being. Also, there is a general feeling of fullness bordering on decay that is easily associated with *peace*. Neither *violence* nor *peace* in this sense is in accord with the creative transformations through which the more splendid achievements of the universe have taken place. As the distinguished anthropologist A. L. Kroeber once indicated: The ideal situation for any individual or any culture is not exactly "bovine placidity." It is, rather, "the highest state of tension that the organism can bear creatively."

In this perspective the present question becomes not the question of conflict or peace, but how we can deal creatively with these enormous tensions that presently afflict our planet. As Teilhard suggests, we must go beyond the human into the universe itself and its mode of functioning. Until the human is understood as a dimension of the earth, we have no secure basis for understanding any aspect of the human. We can understand the human only through the earth. Beyond the earth, of course, is the universe and the curvature of space. This curve is reflected in the curvature of the earth and finally in that pyschic curve whereby the entire universe reflects back on itself in human intelligence.

This binding curve that draws all things together simultaneously produces with the inner forces of matter that expansive tension whereby the universe and the earth continue on their creative course. Thus the curve is sufficiently closed to hold all things together while it is sufficiently open to continue emergence into the future. This tenuous balance between collapse and explosion contains the larger mystery of that functional cosmology which provides our most profound understanding of our human situation, even if it does not bring it within reach of our rational processes.

In this context our discussion of peace might well be understood primarily in terms of the Peace of Earth. This is not simply *Pax Romana* or *Pax Humana,* but *Pax Gaia,* the Peace of Earth, from the ancient mythic name for the planet.

We can understand this Peace of Earth, however, only if we understand that the earth is a single community composed of all its geological, biological, and human components. The Peace of Earth is indivisible. In this context the nations have a referent outside themselves for resolving their difficulties. The earth fulfills this role of mediator in several ways. First, the earth is a single organic reality that must survive in its integrity if it is to support any nation on the earth. To save the earth is a necessity for every nation. No part of the earth in its essential functioning can be the exclusive possession or concern of any nation. The air cannot be nationalized or privatized; it must circulate everywhere on the planet to fulfill its life-giving function anywhere on the planet. It must be available for the nonhuman as well as for the human lifeforms if it is to sustain human life. So it is with the waters on the earth. They must circulate throughout the planet if they are to benefit any of the lifeforms on the planet.

Second, we must understand that the Peace of Earth is not some fixed condition, but a creative process activated by polarity tensions requiring a high level of endurance. This creative process is not a clearly seen or predetermined pattern of action; it is rather a groping toward an ever more complete expression of the numinous mystery that is being revealed in this process. Groping implies a disquiet, an incompleteness; it also has the excitement of discovery, ecstatic transformation, and the advance toward new levels of integration.

This Peace of Earth is never quite the same from

one period to another. In its prehuman period it is different from its expression in its human period. In its tribal period, too, this Peace of Earth is expressed in the ritual and poetry and patterns of living that are integral with the natural phenomena. The Peace of Earth in the classical civilizational period is articulated in a more elaborate human-earth and interhuman relationship. In the period of the great industrial empires, the Peace of Earth was massively disturbed in the plundering of the earth and the more deadly weaponry of war. At that time an effort was made to build a new world, functioning not by the ever-renewing spontaneities of nature, but by the use of nonrenewable resources. An effort was made to substitute a peace of human contrivance for the peace of an integral human presence to the earth community in its organic functioning. Now, in the early phases of the post-industrial period, the outlines of an integral ecological community appear.

A third aspect of the Peace of Earth is its progressive dependence on human decision. Presently this human decision is being made dominantly by the industrialized nations in both economics and politics. The severe tensions existing among the great powers are of a planetary order of magnitude because the resolution of these tensions is leading to a supreme achievement: the global unity toward which all earthly developments were implicitly directed from the beginning. This unity would be a final expression of the curvature of space: the return of the earth to itself in conscious reflection on itself.

A fourth aspect of this Peace of Earth is its hopefulness. Evidence for this hopefulness is found in the sequence of crisis moments through which the universe and, especially, the planet Earth have passed from the beginning until now. At each state of its development, when it seems that an impasse has been reached, most improbable solutions have emerged that enabled the Earth to continue its development. At the very beginning of the universe, the rate of expansion had to be at an infinitesimally precise rate so that the universe would neither explode nor collapse. So it was at the moment of passage out of the radiation stage: only a fragment of matter escaped antimatter annihilation, but out of that fragment has come the galactic systems and the universe entire. So at the shaping of the solar system: if the Earth were a little closer to the sun, it would be too hot; if slightly more distant, it would be too cold. If closer to the moon, the tides would overwhelm the continents; if more distant, the seas would be stagnant and life development could not have taken place. So with the ra-